SPOT-THE-DIFFERENCES AROUND THE WORLD

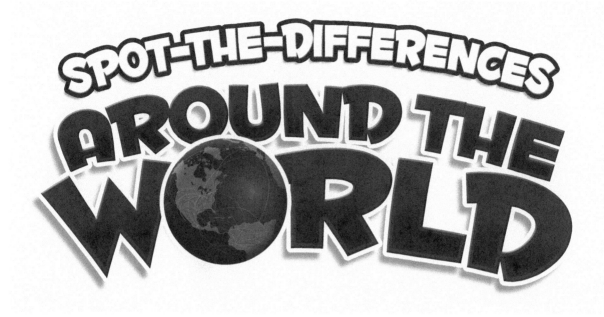

TONY J. TALLARICO

The Empire State Building is a skyscraper located in New York City. The building has 102 stories, and is the tallest building in New York State.

Spot and circle 15 things that are different between these two pictures of the Empire State Building.

DOVER PUBLICATIONS, INC.
MINEOLA, NEW YORK

Bibliographical Note

Spot-the-Differences Around the World is a new work, first published
by Dover Publications, Inc., in 2009.

International Standard Book Number
ISBN-13: 978-0-486-47304-8
ISBN-10: 0-486-47304-X

Manufactured in the United States by RR Donnelley
47304X07   2016
www.doverpublications.com

NOTE

Have you ever wanted to travel around the world? With this unique activity book you can take a trip to twenty interesting locations and landmarks from North and South America, Europe, Asia, Africa, and Australia. Visit the Amazon River Basin, the Eiffel Tower, the Great Wall of China, the Leaning Tower of Pisa, the Parthenon, and other exotic attractions.

Each activity consists of two pictures facing each other. On the left is the original picture, and opposite it on the right is a similar picture—except for the fact that fifteen things in the original picture are different! Look carefully at both pictures and spot the fifteen differences as you go along. For example, in the first pair of pictures, pages 4 and 5, you'll see the Amazon River Basin. There is a parrot in the lower left hand corner of the left-hand picture. The parrot does not appear in the right-hand picture, so draw a circle around the space where he should appear on page 5. When you have spotted and circled fifteen items on a page, you're ready to move on to the next set of pictures. There's a Solutions section beginning on page 44, if you want to check your work.

The Amazon River Basin is home to the largest rainforest on earth.
It covers about 40% of the South American continent and includes part of
eight countries. It is home to millions of insects, plants, birds and mammals.

Spot and circle 15 things that are
different between these two pictures
of the Amazon River Basin.

Famous for keeping impeccable time, the Big Ben Clock Tower is located in London, England. The name Big Ben refers to the 14-ton bell located inside the tower.

Spot and circle
15 things that are
different between these
two pictures of the
Big Ben Clock Tower.

The CN tower in Toronto, Ontario, Canada is a communications and observation tower that stands about 1,815 feet tall! It is the tallest free-standing structure in North America, and is considered one of the seven wonders of the modern world.

Spot and circle 15
things that are different
between these two
pictures of the CN Tower.

The Polynesian island located in the southeastern Pacific Ocean,
called Easter Island, is famous for its monumental statues, called
moai. The statues were created by the *Rapanui* people to honor
their dead chiefs and other important people.

Spot and circle 15 things that
are different between these two
pictures of Easter Island.

Located on the Seine River in Paris, France, the Eiffel Tower was originally designed as the entrance arch for *Exposition Universelle*, a world's fair commemorating the centennial of the French Revolution.

Spot and circle
15 things that
are different
between these
two pictures of
the Eiffel Tower.

The Empire State
Building is a
skyscraper located
in New York City.
The building has
102 stories, and
is the tallest
building in
New York State.

Spot and circle 15 things that are different between these two pictures of the Empire State Building.

The 93-ton bronze statue of the Great Buddha of
Kamakura, Japan, was once housed inside of a temple.
The temple was destroyed by a tsunami, but the
statue has survived outdoors ever since.

Spot and circle 15 things that are
different between these two pictures
of the Great Buddha of Kamakura.

The Great Sphinx of Giza stands on the west bank of the Nile River near Cairo, Egypt. The ancient statue of a lion with a human head stands 241 feet long, 20 feet wide, and 65 feet high.

Spot and circle 15 things that are different between
these two pictures of the Great Sphinx of Giza.

The Great Wall of China stretches over approximately four-thousand miles, and was built in order to protect the northern borders of the Chinese Empire from attacks.

Spot and circle 15 things that are different between these two pictures of the Great Wall of China.

The Leaning Tower of Pisa is the bell tower of the cathedral in the city of Pisa, Italy.
Although the tower stood straight when it was built in 1173,
it began leaning soon after its construction.

Spot and circle 15 things that are different between these two pictures of the Leaning Tower of Pisa.

IN THIS TEMPLE
AS IN THE HEARTS OF THE PEOPLE
FOR WHOM HE SAVED THE UNION
THE MEMORY OF ABRAHAM LINCOLN
IS ENSHRINED FOREVER

Built to honor the sixteenth president of the Unites States,
Abraham Lincoln, the Lincoln Memorial is located on the National Mall,
Washington D.C. Over 3.6 million tourists visit the memorial every year.

IN THIS TEMPLE
AS IN THE HEARTS OF THE PEOPLE
FOR WHOM HE SAVED THE UNION
THE MEMORY OF ABRAHAM LINCOLN
IS ENSHRINED FOREVER

Spot and circle 15 things that are different between
these two pictures of the Lincoln Memorial.

The Little Mermaid Statue sits on a rock in Copenhagen Harbor at Langelinie, Denmark. It symbolizes the famous fairy tale by Danish poet and author, Hans Christian Andersen.

Spot and circle 15 things that are different between these two pictures of the Little Mermaid Statue.

Neuschwanstein Castle, or New Swan Castle, is a
19th century palace in southwest Bavaria, Germany.
The castle, which receives about 6,000 visitors per day,
was the inspiration for Disneyland's Sleeping Beauty Castle.

Spot and circle 15 things that are different between
these two pictures of Neuschwanstein Castle.

Located in Athens, Greece, the Parthenon is a temple built in the 5th century B.C. It was originally designed to be seen only from the outside—people were not permitted inside, and could only glimpse the interior statues through open doors.

Spot and circle 15 things that are different
between these two pictures of the Parthenon.

The Pyramid of the Sun is the third largest pyramid in the world and the largest structure in Teotihuacán, an enormous archaeological site in Mexico City. Construction on this pyramid began around 100 A.D., and it is believed to have represented a major deity.

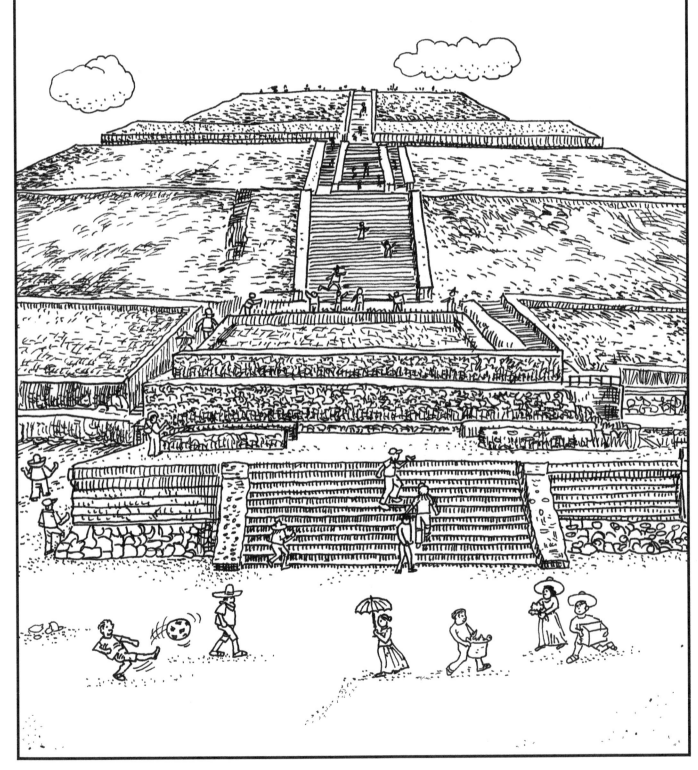

Spot and circle 15 things that are different between
these two pictures of the Pyramid of the Sun.

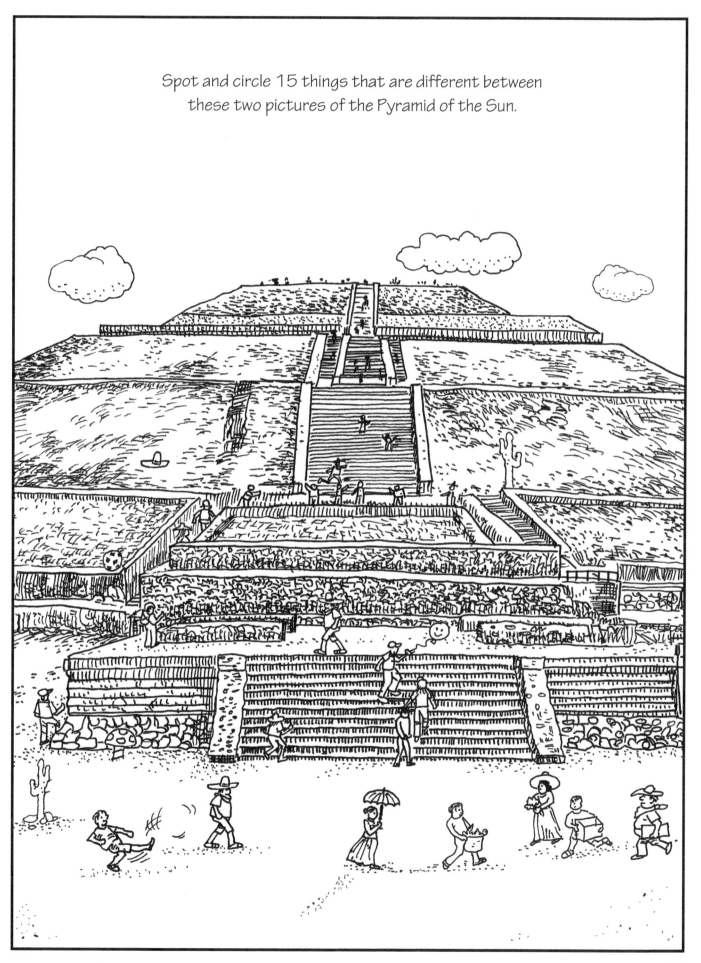

St. Basil's Cathedral is located on the Red Square in Moscow, Russia.
Commissioned by Ivan the Terrible, it is now the most recognized
building in Russia because of its onion-shaped domes.

Spot and circle 15 things that are different between
these two pictures of St. Basil's Cathedral.

Stonehenge is a prehistoric monument located in Wiltshire, England. One of the most mysterious sites in the world, archaeologists believe that this stone monument was built over a period of 1,500 years—but it is unknown how or why it was constructed.

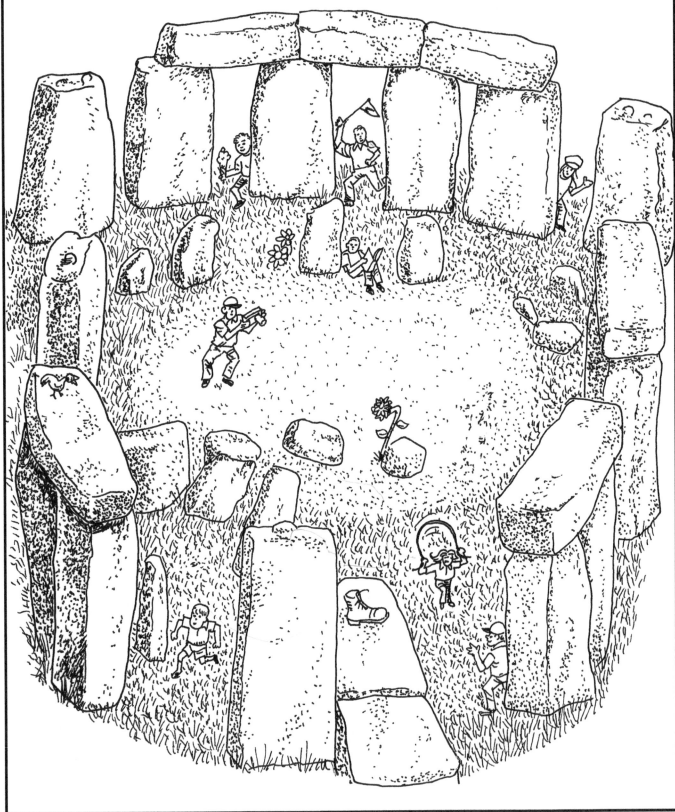

Spot and circle 15 things that are different between these two pictures of Stonehenge.

Located in Sydney, Australia, the Sydney Opera House is a multi-venue performing arts center. It was opened in 1973, and is considered one of the great iconic buildings of the 20th century.

Spot and circle 15 things that are different between these
two pictures of the Sydney Opera House.

The Taj Mahal, located in Agra, India, is a mausoleum built by the Emperor Shah Jahan in memory of his favorite wife. It took twenty thousand workers and over one thousand elephants about twelve years to complete.

Spot and circle 15 things that are different between
these two pictures of the Taj Mahal.

The Netherlands, a country located in the northwestern part of Europe, is well known for its windmills. Originally built to grind grain, today many of them are used to generate electricity, or as windpumps to control flooding.

Spot and circle 15 things that are different
between these two pictures of a windmill.

SOLUTIONS

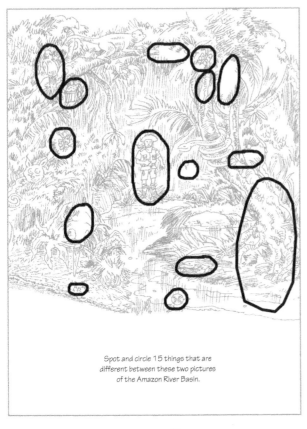

Spot and circle 15 things that are different between these two pictures of the Amazon River Basin.

page 5

Spot and circle 15 things that are different between these two pictures of the Big Ben Clock Tower.

page 7

Spot and circle 15 things that are different between these two pictures of the CN Tower.

page 9

Spot and circle 15 things that are different between these two pictures of Easter Island.

page 11

Spot and circle 15 things that are different between these two pictures of the Eiffel Tower.

page 13

Spot and circle 15 things that are different between these two pictures of the Empire State Building.

page 15

Spot and circle 15 things that are different between these two pictures of the Great Buddha of Kamakura.

page 17

Spot and circle 15 things that are different between these two pictures of the Great Sphinx of Giza.

page 19

Spot and circle 15 things that are different between these two pictures of the Great Wall of China.

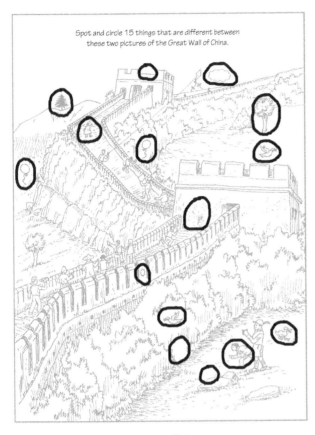

page 21

Spot and circle 15 things that are different between these two pictures of the Leaning Tower of Pisa.

page 23

IN THIS TEMPLE
AS IN THE HEARTS OF THE PEOPLE
FOR WHOM HE SAVED THE UNION
THE MEMORY OF ABRAHAM LINCOLN
IS ENSHRINED FOREVER

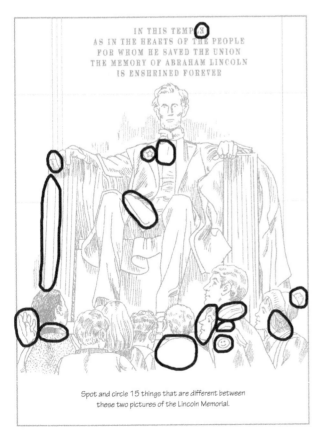

Spot and circle 15 things that are different between these two pictures of the Lincoln Memorial.

page 25

Spot and circle 15 things that are different between these two pictures of the Little Mermaid Statue.

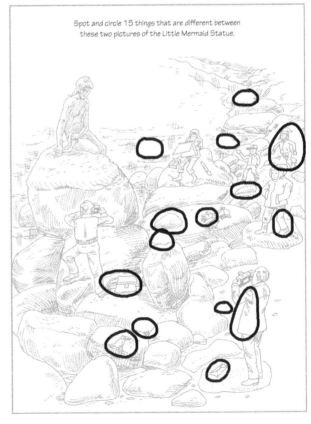

page 27

Spot and circle 15 things that are different between these two pictures of Neuschwanstein Castle.

page 29

Spot and circle 15 things that are different between these two pictures of the Parthenon.

page 31

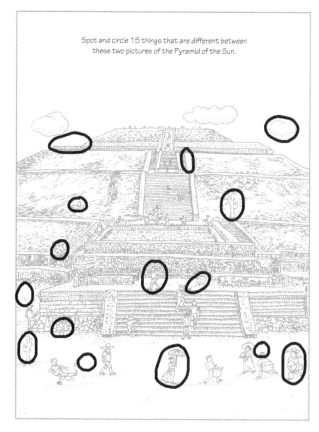

Spot and circle 15 things that are different between these two pictures of the Pyramid of the Sun.

page 33

Spot and circle 15 things that are different between these two pictures of St. Basil's Cathedral.

page 35

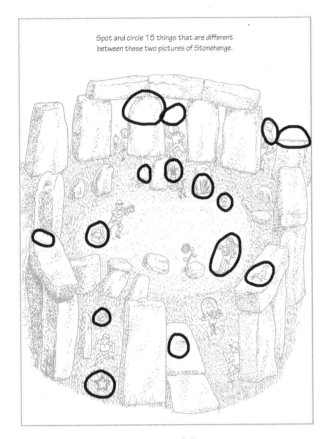

Spot and circle 15 things that are different between these two pictures of Stonehenge.

page 37

Spot and circle 15 things that are different between these two pictures of the Sydney Opera House.

page 39

Spot and circle 15 things that are different between these two pictures of the Taj Mahal.

page 41

Spot and circle 15 things that are different between these two pictures of a windmill.

page 43